A DAY
IN THE
REPUBLIC

TIM SUERMONDT

DOS MADRES

2025

DOS MADRES PRESS INC.
P.O. Box 294, Loveland, Ohio 45140
www.dosmadres.com   editor@dosmadres.com

Dos Madres is dedicated to the belief that the small press is essential
to the vitality of contemporary literature as a carrier of the new voice,
as well as the older, sometimes forgotten voices of the past. And in an
ever more virtual world, to the creation of fine books pleasing to the
eye and hand.

Dos Madres is named in honor of Vera Murphy and Libbie Hughes,
the "Dos Madres" whose contributions have made this press possible.

Dos Madres Press, Inc. is an Ohio Not For Profit Corporation and a
501 (c) (3) qualified public charity. Contributions are tax deductible.

Executive Editor: Robert J. Murphy

Illustration & Book Design: Elizabeth H. Murphy
www.illusionstudios.net

Typeset in Adobe Garamond Pro & Warnock Pro
ISBN 978-1-962847-42-1
Library of Congress Control Number: 2025948394

ACKNOWLEDGEMENTS

Many thanks to the editors of the following Journals where some of these poems have been previously published.

Atlanta Review
The Field Guide to Poetry
Cider Press Review
Innisfree Poetry Journal
Hole in the Head—anthology for Ukraine
The Fortnightly Review (England/France)
Third Wednesday
Scud
Bindweed (Ireland)
Otoliths
Henniker Review
Visions-International
Sisyphus Magazine
Offcourse Journal
Obsessed With Pipework (England)
Read Carpet (USA/Columbia)
Constellations
Poetry Porch
Orchards Poetry Review
Lily Poetry Review
Amethyst Journal (England)
Poetry Breakfast
Nixes Mate Review
Divot
Alabama Literary Review
Berlin Literary Review
Ocean State Review
Literary Yard
Slant
Amsterdam Review
Poetry Salzburg

for Pui Ying
and in memory, Connie Norgren

Before dawn, a dog barks,
then the angels begin to whisper

—Max Jacob

TABLE of CONTENTS

1

2

4

A DAY IN THE REPUBLIC

WHO

I was convinced it was an omen,
seeing the owl on a plank
in the apartment complex—
wisdom, wisdom.

Making my way to the diner
for an evening soup and sandwich
I thought of how this wisdom
might manifest itself—

could it possibly be strong enough
to save me, save the world?
That's asking for a lot from wisdom,
but I trusted my instincts,

now that I was on the verge
of a sharp increase in intellectual heft.
I said to the moon *Be nice*,
great things are coming—wisdom, wisdom.

THE CITY

I walk around it
as if I didn't have a care,
holding every care at bay.
I do have a packed suitcase

in the closet of my apartment,
ready for any emergency
though I have no desire to ever
leave. I love the city, and it loves

me, nonsensical as that must sound
to those who aren't in love.
In the park by the lake I'm still
amazed by the odd but beautiful

peach and pear trees and on clear
days how the sky hovers over
the tall buildings like a blue painting
and how the sunlight bathes the ground

and all the city's inhabitants.
Before I get on a tram I always say
goodbye with a quick wave, never
knowing exactly when I'll return.

KENNEDY'S

A good friend is animated tonight
because he thinks he's in love,
dares to think this time it will be
reciprocated. The clamor at the bar

matches the clamor of the city—
this is where we go to take stock,
to repair, to celebrate even better.
All the voices that insist they can change

the world and themselves, words
and beer on lips beautiful and on lips
chapped hard by having to come
from behind just to hang on for dear life—

the photos of the martyred president
watch us from the walls, lamps shining
like little moons, my good friend
luminous in his rumpled suit of beginning.

SHALLOW HARBOR

The boat brings my wife and I
to the shore.
We grab our one suitcase
and walk over a series of wooden
planks that keep us
from stepping in mud and on
the tiny, strange creatures that inhabit it.
We don't know where we're going.
My wife points at a fleet of crows
flying fast.
"Let's go in their direction," she says,
and we do. Even though I'm aware
it's dangerous
to look back, I take a glance.
The city whose skyline I should be able
to see is not there, gone completely.
I'll miss
the streetlights most of all,
the sad yet romantic illumination
I bathed myself in for decades.
My wife and I follow a dirt road,
leading to
the future we can't trust but cherish.
The crows circle nearby
when we kiss.

ARMIES

I finished the book,
put it on the nightstand,
turned off the lamp and went to sleep.

A ferocious mountain of dust
was coming ever closer, the outline
of sinister vehicles taking the lead.

I woke, turned on the lamp,
picked up the book, checking again
for the balm at the end:

"And the army retreated in the same dust
they had kicked up when they arrived."
I felt relieved, for all of us.

HEADING FOR A BOOKSTORE

when I stop on this sunny day
to watch boxers putting on an exhibition
in the Tuileries, two Frenchmen
smaller than Sonny Liston's arms.
It's a festive and gentlemanly match,
no one in the crowd will see blood
and bruises—a boy up front in a crouch
is jabbing and punching harder.
I slip between people, continuing on,
doing a little rope-a-dope down the boulevard
as I near the bookstore, taking my time
to make a sharp entrance into the ring I love.

ST. PATRICK'S DAY, 2022

The last bottle of Guinness
is rescued from the refrigerator—

the luck of the Irish salvaging
what's possible. Sadness does pervade

the air, but hope butts its way in
with an aggression it didn't know it had

and it doesn't even apologize.
Someone is lost in a train station, a couple

dream of going to Paris *one day, one day*—
the last bottle of Guinness is poured into

glasses, devoutly like a priest who passes
the cheers in the form of a blessing.

WE ALL MOVE ON, SOMEHOW

Francis tells me he's closing down
the hardware store—after 25 years,
the last five with me as a customer.

"Just don't have enough to go on."
"Can I still buy a big wrench set today," I say,
trying a little positivity. "Buy three," he says

"and I'll kiss you on the cheek."
I buy two and he still insists on giving
me a discount. I thank him and he thanks me,

sunlight on the cash register. I carry my wrench sets,
one under each arm, thinking I'm set for life,
ready to repair anything the world keeps breaking.

THE OUTLOOK

The doctor says my heart is strong
"No problem."

Hearing the results over the intercom
the nurses rhumba on all floors,
patients of every malady joining
in or cheering them on.

A marching band turns onto a busy street,
the drivers honking away, in favor.

A storm on the verge of bursting slinks
back to hide behind the clouds, the clouds
themselves making lanes for the sunrays
to douse the proceedings in yellow.

Is the world coming to me, or am I
coming to it, faithful heart in hand. Either way
No problem.

CAMBRIDGE STREET

I walk the hospital corridor
one last time before my release
this morning, my slippers
cruising over the floor, the wax

now a smooth silk of gold.
I can see the birch trees and the blooming
everywhere, cheering up the windows
immaculate in their cleanliness.

The woman in the room next to mine
has beaten me by a couple of hours,
how I was wishing we would leave together,
how I wanted her to meet my wife

who's on her way, carrying a shirt
and a pair of pants and one red rose
she told me she would bring, long-stemmed
like longevity for all the days to come.

MY FAME

How surprising to bump into her
on Queens Boulevard, right in front
of the scuffed courthouse.
It's been years since we parted,
years since we failed to conquer
the city together as we believed—
the new world unable to topple the old.
We didn't say a word, kept walking on
under a bright sun that had brought
many of us out,
but we did look back for an instant,
neither waving nor mouthing good luck.
I felt the subway rumble beneath me
and on this most ordinary day I wondered
who my fame was seeing now,
if she and her latest companion
were as dashing as we once imagined we were,
huddled in a tiny apartment above the bodega.

THE METROPOLITAN MUSEUM

I whisk through the Egyptian exhibit—
we know each other well, no need
for acknowledging.
I head for the small modern art stalls—
strangeness, absurdity and silliness,
how can I stay away? Something
that isn't is and something that
is isn't. I wonder
what Ramses would think of these rooms.
Here's a piece featuring a bus spinning
on a record player, the sky a cauldron
of yellow, the blackbirds unfazed
and down a bit to the left
a museum guard has rabbits peeking
out of his uniform—which causes me
to check my pockets,
nothing alive, keys and wallet lonely still.

NIGHT TURNING

The lights from the office buildings
shine too faintly to faze the darkness.

In my study I'm working on a poem
about irretrievable loss,

but I can't get it written, the poem becoming
more hopeful and gentle with every line.

The night picks up the slack of the lights,
settling so beautifully around my little desk.

THIS MORNING

When the tragedy of the world
became personal this morning,
it did take me by surprise
and immediately after the news
I stood at the window, looking
at the swath of sunflowers
that seemed to have grown overnight
in the park pushing into summer,
the sun perfect in its allotment
of light and heat, the kind of day
I would have loved without reservation,
a day I would have loved seeing you
again among the birds, the high-rises,
in the city you said you'd never leave.

ONE OF THESE DAYS TOO
—for Lee

There *is* a mathematical bent
to the world, a precision

despite the chaos, quite strange
but we poets encompass multitudes,

well… we do the best we can.
As I rummage through every facet

of the city, tabulating this and that,
there's no agenda, no gnashing of teeth,

the heart full and meek today.
Under a department store awning

Pythagoras stands, spiffy in his captain's
uniform, the great river waiting right

around the corner, sailboats and their
geometry on sleepy, grateful display.

I count my steps and the number of birds
leading to the water's edge.

I'LL TAKE THE MOMENT

The day is at its zenith—
the sun benign and everyone
in the city headed for lunch.

I walk from the courthouse
to the river and back, marveling
at my steps that feel lighter than air.

Not everything is right, it never
is, but there's no stopping me now,
the world in a cap tagging along.

BEFORE THE NOW

I waited for my wife-to-be
in front of a bookstore
in a city of dying bookstores.

When I saw her in the distance
she seemed to be getting taller
and more beautiful with each step,

a charming giant by arrival time.
I glanced at the display window,
just to see if my book was there.

It wasn't. It wasn't—love can only
do almost everything. Excuse me,
my wife, holding a book, is here now.

OPEN BOULEVARD

The night rides its moonlight cover
and the city and its inhabitants

are rolled up in its folds. Not to worry,
there's plenty of life still inside

starting with marigolds, hammers—shoes
and books that will take you anywhere.

THE DAY IS RELIGIOUS

And an angel on the street
calls for me to come down.

"Don't you mean come up?"
"Just do it," she says, the irritation
in her voice can't be hidden.

I put on my shoes and arrive to find
her gone. I've had it with the mysteries
of religion and decide to get

a bite at the diner, sunlight emerging
over my shoulder like a halo.

THE AGENDA

Amidst the busyness of the city
I buy a hot dog from a street vendor
and eat it slowly on my way home.

My wife having arrived ahead of me
will be simmering a healthier fare.

I pick up my steps when I see myself
falling into her arms and the last
bite of the hot dog feels exquisite.

If I were any happier they'd have
to arrest me—they know where I live.

TO MY BUDDHIST FRIENDS

I insist on having baggage
so I can't be one of you,
and some things you've accepted
I won't.

I admire quiet, but I don't love it.
I need some bustle, the bustle of a city,
even if it's
merely a pizzeria by a busy bus station.

But I know you haven't given up on me
so let me be charitable
and wind down with a koan of my own:
Why is this

beautiful day not enough
while a tiny white spider crawls
the kitchen wall?
Okay, dear friends, it's enough.

HIS LAST BOOK

Can't be, not yet, too early
though he had milage.

Terrific writers are not
supposed to die, though
they do, often slipping
out without a word.

When I heard the news
I sat down for a few minutes,
though I was restless
and not sure as to why.

I got up to start dinner
early or was it late. I thought
I saw him flying slowly

by the windows, though
I knew this couldn't be.

I set a plate for him anyway
and took that last book
from the shelves and heard
my wife's keys opening

the front door, the normal sound
I'd heard often, though
this time I heard his faint
knock as well, his first and final.

THE WORLD BECOMES BEARABLE

When the dog shedding its fear of water

jumps into the fountain moat

to rescue a child's rubber baseball.

When a group of women in cherry black

dresses spread out a tri-colored

picnic basket underneath an ancient oak.

When lovers pop-up like magic, reminding

you why you wave Love's banner

as the answer to every question.

When the sun rises and sets, in between

no politician does anything dreadful

and your notebook lives with possibilities again.

When the night is so quiet you can hear

the angels around your bed whispering.

NIGHT FISHING

The moon seems to be doing nothing tonight.
I know the moon always seems to be doing
nothing, but that knowledge is even more acute now:

standing at the window of my study I think
of my father and I night fishing for the first and last
time, both of us giving up early, having caught no fish,

absolute zero, a poor physics, some fishermen we were.
I see a man on the park's pathway holding aloft
a good-sized fish for the world to see. The tricks the light

and your mind can play on you is endless.
But keep doing nothing, moon. You're beautiful.

SENIORITY

I walk with my father,
my older steadiness
helping his old unsteadiness.
He slips a few times,

but my grip makes him
fall proof. "It never used
to be this hard," he says,
refusing to walk even slower.

"Apple trees, I like apple
trees"—I don't see any,
though I tell him we'll pick
everyone of them clean later.

Back in the apartment he slides
into his favorite chair, caressing
the arms, staring into space—
what exactly does he see?

I bring him a blanket, but he
waves it off. "Just bring me an apple
for dinner. I could eat a horse."
It's the kind of logic I've come to love.

BOYS

The old man walks
with his wooden cane.

Right beside him is a boy
carrying a skateboard

almost longer than he is.
They seem a most compatible

couple, talking and laughing.
From the beginning of A

to the end of Z, everyday
they're on their way to eternity.

SAFE

My father is starting
his final journey, in the emergency ward,
and there I am, leaning over him

with my awkward concern, listening
for the first words he'll say once he sees me:
"Did you lock the door before you left?"

How I've admired his skill, his genius for detail
and how embarrassed I've been, many times,
by my wayward approach to such serious attention.

But I did lock the door to my apartment,
all the possessions, the few treasures safe.
I show my father the keys.

A TUESDAY

Alone, thinking of you,
I watch the construction workers
assembling the building walls,
some scampering like ants yet
in control with a surprising precision—
until the sky opens up, dropping
buckets of rain the forecast missed.
We're both probably done for the day,
although I try to rivet a line only
to delete it quickly and close my literary
box of tools—tomorrow for me,
tomorrow for the workers, tomorrow
when we both will see you arrive,
dry and beautiful, the work important again.

TOGETHER

It's starting to rain hard
and the homeless man
who's living in the neighborhood
offers me his umbrella
shredded quite profusely.
I take it and give it back
to him as mine. We'd
make a great comedy pair,
he says, and for a moment
we are pals, forgetting
the rain, how silly we look
getting soaked under it together.

THE HIGHEST GRADE

A man shouts from across the street
"You're my hero!"
and for a moment I think his words

are directed at me.
Well, why not? I must have done
some small heroic things in my life

and, surely, all my loved ones
believe me capable of great heroics.
When I realize I am not the person

intended, I put my hands
in my light spring jacket,
take a few steps and see a man helping

an elderly woman cross the crowded street.
Different woman, different street
but I did just that last week,

that tiny decency. We linked arms
and made it safely to the entrance
of her grand, blue building.

SIMPLICITY

It's what we all want,
even for those writers who would rather
jump off a tall building
than admit that truth. Reams of complexity,
the kind that makes the poor reader's
eyes glaze over quickly, can always find
an enabler to tell you its brilliance,
but one gooey word in a work that claims
simplicity can bring the whole edifice down.
My simplicity, such as it is, is like a dinghy
on a sea of battleships and aircraft carriers.
I float unencumbered by guns and planes,
no need for enablers of any kind. The vastly
more dangerous route suits me just fine.

PISSARRO KEEPS IT GOING

The woman, seemingly not bothered
wearing a dress of several folds
in the summer's heat, stands at the edge
of a little hill, surveying the village,
the fields, the larger hills in the distance
bright green against the chalk-blue sky.
She might be wondering about a thousand
things at once, like I've done and keep doing,
wondering as the world moves in, pulls away,
playing at being intimate, hard to get.
We must both be in love now, impossible
imagining the two of us not forever linked,
standing in our small place while the universe
blooms all around us, large and less lonely.

CHARTRES

At the South Portal
two house painters across
the narrow and rutted dirt road
sit on an outcropping of rocks,
each one eating a sandwich.

Standing near the stern, elongated
Martyrs in stone I give the painters
a *Bonjour* and they do the same,
lifting their long sandwiches like
a sword in greeting.

The temptation to ask the Martyrs
to come to life and join us is as strong
as it is silly, but if the miraculous
is not here, where is it, and why not
invite them out of simple kindness.

Same for the Apostles at attention,
even for Christ who doesn't seem
to be enjoying his stone perch, ready
to appear again as a man to bless us
and the sandwiches that look so good.

CHECKING THE SCORE AND SIMONE WEIL

It is odd that I'm thinking of her
as I'm thinking too of the big football game,
the pizza I'll be eating in front of the television

as I watch men's bodies collide in violence and poetry,
Weil's sturdy contradictions exposing my shallowness—
oh I know, I'm hopeless, completely.

George Orwell once remarked on some ideas being
so absurd only an intellectual could believe them.
I admire the notion, but I wish I were an intellectual—

a man whose mind is deemed *exquisite and imposing*
by his allies and enemies alike—one who has the wisdom
to sneak out of grand soirees, check the score

in the cool air of the night and pray his team hold on
to a healthy lead or rally from a difficult deficit.
"Love needs reality." Like my team and I need a win.

RECKONING

Light snow on the train tracks,
spring just around the bend,

the roar of the city, rhythms of birdsongs,
traumas of the past drowning
in an ocean of flames,

entertainment, dancing and singing,
an unfinished poem on the study's table,
all nestled in a house's sanctuary,

a woman in the kitchen, draped in a bathrobe,
lighting a cigarette in happy defiance.

WE MAY, EVENTUALLY, GET WHAT WE WANT

Wet outside,
but the construction workers
are carrying on: digging, raising, attaching…

exactly what I'm trying to do
with poems in my dry study—
both of us refusing to allow

the Muse and Nature
to bedevil us into abandonment.
Months, a year from now,

we'll be able to be pleased with our efforts,
finding compassion for having been so hard
on ourselves—we did the best

we could and anyway no one is supreme,
or as a character on an old
Western tv show put it: "Only God is supreme"

and, trust me, He's had his shaky
episodes as well.
Despair and its consiglieres don't win

every day—look at the beautiful commodity
of the buildings, of the words holding on
for dear life.

PAINTING A BOSTON NOIR

No amount of brushstrokes
can cover over the ubiquitous brown,

not even by inserting street lamps
and a yellow bird flying between them.

A man, his head down, is walking
one of those streets, trying to feel whole,

adroit in the world once again, the neon
sign of the donut shop with its missing

letter hanging like a failed omen, a regret
that will haunt the seeker who expected

at least the crumbs of a miracle. The moon
isn't painted in, tomorrow night perhaps.

MENASHE

He wrote short poems
like I like to do,
even writing shorter poems
than my short poems.
Short poems can be scattered
easily, but cover more territory.
Look, there's a short poem
falling from the leaves
like a drop of rain. Oh you
beautiful poem, beautiful leaves,
beautiful rain. You can borrow
my blue raincoat, Samuel.

PASSY

I buy an ice cream
and go back into the park for the first

time in many, many years.
Everything has changed and nothing has—

A most interesting phenomenon.
An old man helps an even older man

to walk, a young couple are mesmerized
by each other, and there I am, a boy

carrying a stack of books—
what on earth was I thinking?

But history has yet to figure out
what to do with me, so there's hope

for a surprise, maybe in a decade
where miniature stars drop on rooftops

on their way to falling around my feet,
and all I can do is look up in wonder.

NEAR THE EDGE OF A NEW YEAR

I'm older

but still bumbling and stumbling

through the world like I did

when I was younger.

The coming days will provide

comfort so far as the sentiments

show heart, my friends who left

too fast alive in the magic of memory,

a church we built against all churches.

Dear friends wherever you are,

may you be bumbling and stumbling

still with me.

A choir a bit out of tune can be beautiful.

FISHERMAN

He decides it's time to make
that faraway move, believing

he can thread his new life
as well as he rigged and maintained

the trawlers for decades. He wraps
up his small drawings of mermaids

he did a while ago—that's over
but he can't leave them behind.

He won't be found tonight in a string
of bars along the waterfront, bars invisibly

tethered to the moon. He'll be in bed
early, dreaming of the coming dawn

while the mermaids on top of his suitcase
bask in the dim light, shining like brides.

THE REPUBLIC

In my dream
I run across a retired,
celebrated quarterback

tossing a football with an old teammate.
"Can I join in?"—my once
cannon arm feeling young again.

"Sure," the quarterback says, "it's still
a democracy." We all ignore
the snow that seems to have arrived

from another dream, the snow that is falling
harder and harder as we throw lovely spirals
endlessly to one another.

HIGH TIME

Still you should praise the spring
—Ha Jin

After all, you remember how romantic
some of your departed friends were—
the sight of a flower blooming could make

them ecstatic. Impossible to burden them
with your qualms about spring—you've
praised flowers too. Today you decide to take

a long walk for them, a day full of sun, birds
and of course flowers, even people spilling
out quietly, one apartment complex after

the other, feeling like painting their front doors
blue to banish the drab olive gray entrances
appreciated only by armies and warlords.

You call the names of friends in your mind
and are happy to hold the conversations there,
their voices overlapping yet lively and splendid.

A little girl by a statue half covered in grime
is dressed as an angel, her mother trying to fix
a wing that fell, the entire world hoping she can.

THE MAGICIAN TRIES

Reaches into his stove-pipe hat,
promising to produce a rabbit.
But he pulls up nothing, tries again
and yet again and still nothing.

The small fairground crowd mumbles,
some laugh, some jeer, and all of them
walk off, leaving the magician crestfallen
and embarrassed, and one suspects

this was not the first time he's failed.
But how often have we seen a rabbit
pulled from a hat, or flowers, and many
objects? Does this really thrill anymore?

Imagine pulling nothing from a hat, again
and yet again. Nothing is something too
and capable of being anything imagined
and written. How magical nothing is.

WHAT WE EXPECT

The man says he talks to the trees
and that they talk to him.
He'd love to tell me what they've said
but he's sworn to never tell anyone.

I think the trees think he's a nuisance,
but they've put up with worse
and let him go on until he's finished
for the day, the week, the month, the year.

Just yesterday I went up to a big tree,
put a hand on one of its limbs
and said: "What would you like to talk about?"
I got no response as I figured,

but I so wanted to hear it say: "Well,
let's talk about your latest poem."
I was prepared had this happened. What we hope
to expect from the world is worth a disappointment.

A SWIRL KEPT MOVING

The early evening is darkening quickly
in a rash of blue—"Egyptian Blue"

my painter friend would have told me.
As I watch the darkening, waiting for

the lights of the city, the bitterness of the day
is receding and foolishness back in play—

if I dance down the boulevard it would be
wonderful in its ornate clumsiness,

the kind I'd make peace with, a deft twirl
surprising me here and there, a swirl

kept moving into dawn—a brightening sky
over the bus lines of another neighborhood.

MATT

He's a tough guy
and how he lights up
whenever he says he is.

He has a Purple Heart
and the Bronze Star.

Only once was he not tough,
he says, when his wife left him
and he bawled for days,

adding while looking at the floor
as if he wanted to burrow beneath
the boards of the bar,

"I was so ashamed." I don't have
anything like the Bronze Star

and yet my wife and I are still madly
in love. I often buy her some flowers,
any battlefield far, far away.

I wonder if he ever bought flowers
for his wife and if he did,

would that have given her second
thoughts about leaving, the sunflowers
on the table begging her to stay as well.

SHE'S GLAD SHE'S HERE

The widow has come out,
her shawl waving a bit in the breeze

as if announcing her return.
Not many people are outside

and her timing pleases her.
She walks past the construction site

and into the park along the river.
She sits on a bench near where she

and her husband liked to spend time,
the huge trees still right overhead.

She looks across the river, to the city
skyline she and her husband marveled at.

She's interrupted by a man who passes
in front of her, carrying a sign that reads:

Repent You won't live forever
"Oh Mister," she says to herself "you can

do a lot better." She takes off her shawl,
putting it on her lap. She's glad she's here.

MORE THAN A WORD

Mercy: a fine word
but I want it to be more than a word.

I want it to be living and purposeful,

a swan on the lake in the park, a man

who's marching with confidence
down the sidewalks despite his broken heart,

a woman who wonders were the best years

have gone yet refuses to be defeated.

Twice a year or so I want to look back
when I'm walking and getting the sense

that mercy is following me, like a dog

who's badly in need of a home where she
and I sit by a fireplace, real or imagined.

FIRST NIGHT SNOW

It arrives like a thief who knows the business,
knows no interference will be forthcoming
and besides, we haven't even a broken-down
blunderbuss to wave menacingly in the air.
It does what it wants, running over the landscape
with nature's white gloves, leaving a few clues
in the following afternoon's rain but not enough
to arrest, bring to trial and convict. Everything
at its mercy with many more forays to come, only
in our dreams do we not surrender, burning it
in the core of the sun, out hands red with delight.

AN IMPORTANCE OF BLUE

The blue sky attacked
the gray sky of the morning
and by the afternoon
the gray sky was completely routed.
An inspiration. So much that I
took my blue pen and scribbled
on the nearest paper I had at hand.
A couple lines of poetry formed
and the poem said *follow me*.
I did and the sky became even bluer.

IMAGINATION

A blue cow once got into
one of my poems
and never made a repeat
appearance in any others,

outside of its mentioning here.

I don't know why it got in
in the first place—was I trying
to show that a sliver
of my heart loved being strange?

It's odd to say, but I wish
I had been more generous,
the way we all want to be generous,
and had the blue cow

back for more, the two of us

in a landscape only I invented—
a landscape that escaped the newscasts
to recall apple trees, a river
and a city, an apron of sky so blue

we fell asleep in a field of golden wheat.

LATER IN THE MORNING

A few pretzels still left in the green bowl.

Bad news and good popping up on the phone alerts.

A poem begging to be written, such pleading.

My wife at her desk, putting *her* poem through its paces.

A shaft of sunlight striking a pillow on the couch.

The low hum of the refrigerator guarding the lunch.

A poster of Einstein falling from the wall, gravity and gravitas.

Every chore to be done pushed back for as long as possible.

A mind focused on the city clear as the bluest ocean.

My father in the park, saluting to no one or to everyone.

PAZ

While reading a book of his essays
I dozed off. It wasn't his fault—
the busyness of the city and of the day
did me in. And in this short nap

I had a short dream of tramping
down a boulevard in Mexico City,
kidding around with Paz and Hemingway—
the three of us fast friends, backslapping

one another, howling how each of us
would win the Noble Prize, how spiffy
we'd look at the podium in Stockholm.
When I woke the book was on the floor—

I apologized to Paz, put it on the coffee
table and stepped into the kitchen, rummaging
the refrigerator for the condiments required
to build a first-class sandwich and then—

hearing Paz in Spanish, saying "Cheer up,
dear friend, two out of three is not bad,"
he meant well as a little joke. I layered on
the mayonnaise, starting my own little triumph.

WHAT WE DO WHEN THE WORLD
DOESN'T DEMAND WE DO ANYTHING

I scribble a line on a piece of paper,
maybe a stanza too—for future reference.
I may use none of them any time soon,
as the lines and stanzas that have gotten backed up

can attest to—orphans with a home
and a hope that one day I will employ them.
I notice a woman in a motorized wheelchair,
her dog keeping pace, stepping quite elegantly.

THIS AMERICAN THINKS OF NERUDA

When the moon is bright and full
and the ships are close enough
to showcase their magnificence.

And let's not forget the women
walking barefoot in the sand, their
summer dresses swirling like a dance.

When I'm back in the city, at my desk,
writing, memories of the world of the sea
will keep me company like Neruda

and all the others on the shelves, mermaids
squeezing out from the pages of books
now and then, singing like newlyweds.

A DAY IN THE REPUBLIC

My wife and I walk the city,
miles and miles, territory

we could traverse blindfolded—
even the new establishments

seem familiar, what exactly
is new under the sun? We make

it back to our front door, in time
to join the dusk as it turns to darkness—

the tiny park almost emptied out,
a police siren, but everyone has been good

and not afraid of asking about justice.
A bit of liquor, cooking on the stove—

my wife and I waiting on the bushel
of stars the weatherman says will come.

NEWTON'S APPLE TREE

Still bright green and lush,
with ripe apples—the story
might be true after all.
I've had assorted fruits

from assorted trees plunk
me on the head, but none
that have been a catalyst
to propel me into immortality.

Not that I'm complaining—
I'm eating an ice cream, people
are walking the narrow streets,
browsing, entering and leaving

stores and restaurants in droves,
helping me remember the world
can be kind too. A magic apple
in an alleyway or lying beside

plum blossoms hanging
from a windowsill, or hovering
over my head at this very second—
and why not, here where much began.

CIGARETTE BREAK

It doesn't matter if you smoke or not,
that's a break you take, it's even sanctioned.
You walk toward the hangar entrance,
the arch of metal rimmed with the reflection
of the sun and you feel as if you're about
to enter a portal, but again, what kind—
Heaven, *Paradise*, and is there a difference?
You watch the planes you helped build
crisscross the vanilla blue sky, but when
you scan the land it seems to get flatter,
going on and on that way in the distance
and you realize another life some were sure
you'd have has gotten too far away from hope—
there's no surgeon in the white smock, no
judge in his chambers, no Hollywood with
beauties swirling about like hordes of leaves.
And yet, as you return to work, the dynamos
of the machines and the men and women
who rev them back up keep winning your
admiration no matter how difficult to admit.
Yes, so much goes wrong, though it always will—
you put on your gloves, the world says *Let's go*.

AUTUMN

Finally, falling like paratroopers,
the leaves are blanketing the ground

and the piles are starting to take shape
and I want to kick and jump into the biggest

heaps, like I did when I was a child,
a rather mischievous one the more I recollect.

The world is a mess, but then it's always been,
tragedies ongoing no matter how I write

against them. Yet soon I'm putting on my shoes,
a light jacket and making the plunge once again,

maybe kicking and jumping less this time
as I reconnoiter the area for the most beautiful

leaf for a most beautiful bookmark.
What have I been waiting for all these years?

HAVING TO WORK HARDER

Spring this year will arrive battered
and even a bursting of flowers

may not be sufficient to jam the tank
barrels, yet I remain ready

to put my winter coat in the closet,
ignoring the coat's sadness, but it

will have its days again. I walk
over the city's slivers of snow, close

to the Charles and flocks of geese,
the sun shining early in anticipation.

MY LITTLE ARMY

When I write today
I let the world sprint by,
knowing I'll catch up
once my words limber up

and put on their marching shoes.
The rain has stopped, the old
windows creaked open
and flags are flying like some

Liberation the newsreels prove
does and has happened.
My words, my little army,
have indeed caught the world

surrendering to a happiness.
A last line of a poem actually
mentions light, all clear,
light, all clear, so inexhaustible.

THE PEACE BLOUSE

Immediately upon delivery
my wife opened the box
and tried on the blouse,

a sparkling blue number
and asked my opinion: "It's
as lovely as you are," buttering
her up with the truth.

No sooner had I said this
than I noticed the flowers
on the windowsill stretching

in her direction and the books
on the table ruffling their pages
as if convinced I'd try
to write something beautiful

about her and the blouse
and the books were seldom wrong.
It wasn't far-fetched for me

to imagine a continent away
clashing armies pausing in mid
battle at the sight of my wife's blouse
waving as flags over every

acre of the contested territory.
For an instant, with her blouse alone
my wife had given us the impossible.

HOTEL ODESSA

On my first morning in Paris
I paused at my apartment window,
holding a croissant and a mug of coffee

and watching people go in and out
of the hotel's entrance, convinced each one
of them was a spy, good and bad—

how the imagination of youth
still clings at the age we should know better.
Minutes later I got fully clothed

and made my way to the hotel's small
lobby, hoping a man with a pronounced
scar or a woman whose beauty is timeless

would show me a folder and say:
"You must get this to the American embassy
in Prague by midnight"—the impossibility

and danger of the task making it divine.
But I wound up sitting on a velvet chair,
retying a shoelace, playing back in my mind

the chance I might have had of saving
some, perhaps all of the world and when
I left I looked both ways down the street.

THE STAR FERRY

She can't imagine being put in dry dock,
her practicality and sea-brined beauty gone.

She can't imagine never again taking
people between Kowloon and Hong Kong Island,

the sun and the moon of all the days crossing the harbor.

She can't imagine no longer being roped in and set free,
the glorious back and forth within minutes.

But above all she can't imagine watching other
vessels sailing by and the alabaster blue of the water,

leaving her and the memory of her in tatters,

can't imagine saying to the seabirds "*I'm lonely.*
Please come to visit me as often as you can."

THE RUNNERS GO BY THE APARTMENT

The ultra-talented leaders,
so skinny and nimble, cruise
with strides that are magnificent to observe.

But I'm waiting to see the runners
who will pass by differently, runners of every shape
who will have many go from running

to jogging to walking, some who will
bend over, their hands grabbing their knees
as if begging the earth to filter up a stream of air,

those laters and last of the pack who ask
how they keep thinking they might win one day—
impossible, impossible, until next year for them,

almost every day for me as I chase the immortal line
with a glass of wine, poor winged sandals on my feet.

ACTION IN THOSE DAYS

Cinema 5, Paris

In the parlance of movies
angles construct the whole—

the streets contract and expand,
rooftops of snow burst into flames,

birds turn into bombers and lovers

roll like casino dice from room to room.

A woman lighting up the boulevard
dissolves into a man who's lost—

he's reading a newspaper, victory

or defeat, the headline a mystery,

a huge factory suddenly a huge dovecote
assaulted by rain and thunder—

blue skies at the blink of an eye,
redemption or at least a chance,

a bright river in beautiful fog, the final

scene, shadows and trees everywhere.

FOR CONSTANCE OF THE CITY

One of these nights I'll go looking for you,
even while knowing you can't be found

in this life anymore. I'll scour every street
large and small, following the lights

and the brilliant pulsing of the moonflowers.
And when I finally let the impossible go

I'll return to where I live, waiting for the morning
and the arrival of workers of every stripe,

watching especially for the yellow school buses
that will stop at the corner whitened by a thin

layer of snow, the shadows of the construction
cranes bowing, as if thankful for another day.

WHY ANYTHING IS POSSIBLE

I made every jump shot, every—
that day I was the greatest shooter
in the history of basketball,
the maestro who was automatic
from every angle, every distance,
who wore down the frustrated
and embarrassed defenders early
and often, while every species of birds
known in the area flew overhead,
stopping in mid-flight to stare down,
sensing something extraordinary
was happening—*what human is this?*
When the game was finished I walked
down the streets I knew like my life,
walked not as merely another member
of the neighborhood but in the spirit
of Caesar returning triumphantly from Gaul,
adulation among the crowds at fever pitch,
a Roman sun shining for a Roman son
with no one daring to whisper in his ear
that all glory, all glory, is fleeting—
not on that day of his, not on that day of mine.

GREEN HAIR

The problem vexing me
seemed insurmountable, determined
as I was to find the solution.
I walked to the city to think,

immersing myself in the crowd—how
often I've taken such steps in hope
of clarity. It began to rain, umbrellas
popping up in concert and I ducked

into a dollar store, very little being
only a dollar. A woman with green hair
asked me on what aisle a particular
product might be found. I couldn't help

but told her I liked her green hair,
it was as bright as the summer's grass.
When the rain stopped I left
and silently greeted everyone and everything—

that green hair inexplicably
on my mind, my problem beginning
to crumble, the day suddenly brighter
than ever as I made it home in near triumph.

ALONG THE YELLOW RIVER THE POETS DROP IN

A writer is like a worker with a toolbox.
—Charlie Smith

The fish, large and small, leap up
and land on the plates of the people.
The army marches, carrying flowers
and speaking kindly to the subversives.
The blue birds nearly blanket the sky
and couples commandeer catamarans
to the ends of the earth. Behind curtains
rustling in the cooling breeze the poets
just write, unaware of what it is they've
just done, turning the screws on their
stanzas to make them sturdy and if lucky
beautiful enough to be of use, anywhere.

A TOWN

The buildings arrayed
in dueling facades of medieval,

renaissance and neo—a town
de Sica would have loved.

People share the tight-fitting streets
with compact cars and tiny trucks

that slither back and forth
from the plaza, where a marching

band is parading to commemorate
a conflict's end or maybe

its beginning—a lone veteran salutes.
On a balcony touched by grime

and beauty both over the years
a man in a gray suit and a woman

in a summer dress wave,
how dignified and happy their arms

and hands move, the sea air
wafting between us like perfume.

NOT THAT I SOUGHT IT

Somebody called me an elitist—
which was news to me,
I thought I was light years away
from ever becoming one.

But I accepted the mantle
for a short while—I took my elitist
garbage bags down the elitist hall
and in the elitist trash room

dropped them down the elitist chute
and into the arms of the elitist garbagemen.
On my way to the elitist supermarket
I stopped to tell a group of elitist construction

workers how well their building was progressing.
"It's an elitist thing to say," a man
named Moses said, "but we're damn good
at what we do." I, the temporary elitist, understood.

THE DAY AFTER VALENTINE'S DAY

We're still in love
and all the terrible news of the world
we kept at bay that day, news

that has filtered back in, has not yet
thrown us completely off stride.
My wife and I, holding hands, walk

the city streets, both of us gliding a bit
to our surprise and delight.
We duck into a diner, devour the fries

like the world might end tomorrow.
The sky outside starts to darken.
We've missed the all-day sun of yesterday,

but we'll savor the trip home
with Cupid singing in our ears, oh we know
he's getting tired, but we're still in love.

IT'S COME

The sound of what I thought
were church bells roused me
this morning, odd since there's
no church in the area.

I walked into the living room,
looked out the windows and saw
thousands and thousands of people
gathering, many embracing, some

dancing, some singing and dancing.
I went to turn on the television
and heard the breathless reporter:
"It's come. World Peace is here!"

I opened a window and shouted
to the multitudes below "I love me
and I love all of you," what pathetic
nonsense this would have sounded like

earlier. I felt a bit of a breeze, saw birds
of every color, and welcomed my wife's
footsteps from her notoriously deep slumber.
We stood at the window a long, long time.

THE WORLD WILL SURELY END

while I'm finishing a poem,
the last line smoothed in like butter
on toast.
The day won't be glorious,
but it will be sweet,
the sun out
and just a nip of chill in the air.
I'll be pulled
out the window, sucked
up into the clouds and going from there,
joining so many others,
what traffic!
I often wondered where we would ultimately
wind up, such dreams I had.
And now
I'll know, I'll know if any of them were true.

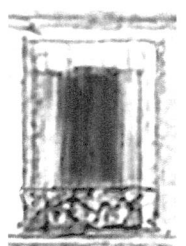

TIM SUERMONDT's sixth full-length book of poems *A Doughnut And The Great Beauty Of The World* came out in 2023 from MadHat Press. He has published in *Poetry, Ploughshares, Prairie Schooner, The Georgia Review, Bellevue Literary Review, Stand Magazine, Smartish Pace, Barrow Street, Amsterdam Review* and *Plume*, among many others. He lives in Cambridge, MA, with his wife, the poet Pui Ying Wong.

www.ingramcontent.com/pod-product-compliance
Lightning Source LLC
Chambersburg PA
CBHW020324130626
46549CB00003B/997